Relocation Workbook

Kids on the Move

by Leah Evans

Illustrated by Cathy Stevens Pratt, Illustration, Design and
Art at catillustrates.com

AFTERSCHOOLPLANS.COM

Who are we?

We are a company dedicated to helping ex-pat children flourish, grow, and learn. We promote American history, education, and happy and flexible living.

Dear Parent,

This book is to help your child transition between a past home and a future home. Record memories, share stories, and paste or draw pictures to remember your past.

We also provide a forum for looking forward and recording hopes, dreams, and expectations for your new home. Make plans about the future to build excitement and enthusiasm for the move. During your first days and weeks, record your thoughts and pictures and compare them with your former home.

This book serves as a keepsake to remember your former home, the transition period, and your first experiences in a new home.

Thank you for purchasing this book.

Sincerely,
www.afterschoolplans.com

Stories to Read about Moving

Alexander, Who's Not (Do You Hear Me? I Mean It!) Going to Move, Judith Viorst, Ray Cruz

Big Ernie's New Home: A Story for Young Children Who Are Moving, Teresa Martin

The Berenstain Bears' Moving Day, Stan and Jan Berenstain

Boomer's Big Day, Constance W. McGeorge

Big Ernie's New Home: A Story for Young Children Who Are Moving, Teresa Martin, Whitney Martin

Saying Good-Bye, Saying Hello...: When Your Family is Moving, Michaelene Mundy

A New House, Jill Wenzelman

Moving Day! Jess Stockham

Katie Moves, Liesbet Slegers

Ellie McDoodle: New Kid in School, Ruth McNally Barshaw

Relocation Tips for Kids

Make sure you say goodbye to your favorite people and places.

Take pictures to remember your favorite things.

Every day, talk with your family about one thing you are excited to learn about your new home.

Research your new home so you know a few things about it.

Talk to other people who have moved and ask them about their experience.

Find a new friend at your new school to help you adjust. Ask a parent to help you do this by writing to your new school.

Have regular family meetings to talk about moving logistics.

Find a way to maintain some routine during the move. For instance, if you usually read every night before bed, continue to do that. Try to find three things you can continue throughout the transition period.

Make a plan so you know what will happen when, and where!

Have your own to-do list.

Ask your parents to assign you with jobs to help with the move. You can label boxes, pack books, or help manage to-do lists.

Make sure you can keep in touch, write down addresses and contact information for your favorite people.

Pack three things to take with you that make wherever you are feel like home. Ideas include stuffed animals, pillows, a favorite blanket, a water bottle, a picture, books, a favorite lamp, or a small rug.

Take lots of pictures of your favorite people and places! Make a memory book with them if you can.

The first few weeks at a new home are the hardest. Make a list of three fun things you want to explore or discover in that time.

Keep a written or drawn journal to record your feelings.

Have "Family Check-In" time daily during the move. Everybody gets to say how they are feeling and what they need from others.

Find a way to make your mark on your new home right away. Put up a sign with your family name, plant a tree, or buy a brightly colored new rug.

My Life

Write down the story of you, your family, and your relatives.

All About Me!

Name:

_____

Age:

_____

Places I have lived:

_____

Family Members:

_____

_____

School:

_____

Grade:

_____

Hobbies:

_____

Favorite Food:

_____

Favorite Book:

_____

Favorite Activity:

_____

Self-Portrait

Family Moving History

Family stories build resilience in children. Write down stories of family transitions here!

_____

_____

Do your parents have any stories about moving?

_____

_____

Did your grandparents ever move to a new home?

_____

_____

Did any of your great-grandparents move to a new home?

_____

_____

Other Family Stories:

_____

_____

_____

_____

_____

My Family Tree
Home is where my family lives...

Picture of my mother

Picture of my father

List where your parents have lived:

_____

_____

_____

_____

_____

_____

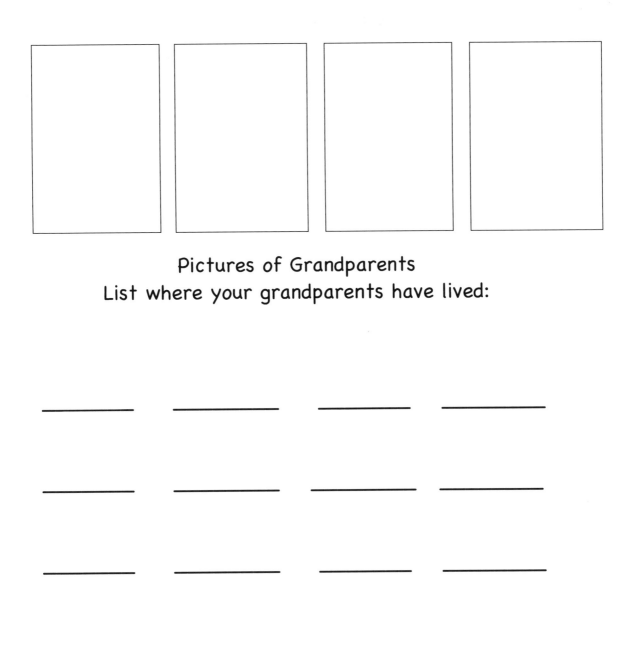

Pictures of Grandparents
List where your grandparents have lived:

_____   _____   _____   _____

_____   _____   _____   _____

_____   _____   _____   _____

_____   _____   _____   _____

Talk to your parents, grandparents, aunts, uncles, and other relatives. Ask for their stories about family members moving to a new home. What is your favorite story? Write it down here (or have an adult help you write it) and then illustrate it.

_____

_____

_____

_____

Can you design a great outfit for kids moving to a new house?

Think about what a moving outfit should be like. Should it be comfortable? Have lots of pockets? Draw a picture of yourself with your perfect moving day outfit below!

Americans on the Move

How have Americans moved to new homes in the past?

1) Thousands of years ago, early Americans traveled to our country by walking over the land bridge from Russia.

2) Hundreds of years ago, the Pilgrims traveled to America on a wooden ship called the Mayflower.

3) Many immigrants came from Ireland, Italy, or Ukraine by boat to New York.

4) Once in America, many people traveled west in the 1800's in Conestoga wagons, searching for new homes and farmland.

5) Many immigrants come to America today by airplane.

6) Americans move to new states using cars, moving vans, or airplanes.

Draw a picture of your favorite form of transportation in the box below. You could choose a car, train, airplane, boat, or anything else that takes you from one place to another!

Old Home

"Old home" means the home you are leaving. "New home" means the home you are going to live in after your move.

Important Information About Our Old Home

Country

_____

Address

_____

Name of our Neighborhood

_____

Name of our School

_____

Favorite Place for Treats

_____

Favorite Food

_____

Favorite Park

_____

Favorite Family Friends

_____

Best Friend

_____

Favorite Smell

_____

Favorite Sight

_____

Favorite Sound

_____

Favorite Season

_____

Picture Page! Paste photographs or draw pictures to remind you of your old home:

My Old Home

Paste a photograph or draw a picture of your home.

Describe your home:

_____

_____

_____

_____

What would your ideal suitcase look like? Decorate an example here!

Map of My Neighborhood

Country:

_____

City:

_____

Neighborhood:

_____

Street:

_____

My Bedroom

Paste a photograph or draw a picture of your room.

Describe your bedroom:

_____

_____

_____

_____

Where have you been, where are you going?

Color the continent where you live and the color where you will be living. Then, list three of your favorite places in the world.

_____

_____

_____

Write a Song about your Move!

Create something fun from your experience. In the left column, write down the words to a simple song or poem that you enjoy. In the right column, change the words to tell the story of your move. Then, sing the song using your words and the melody from the original.

Words to Original Song	Words to Moving Song

My Family in Our Old Home

Paste a photograph or draw a picture of your family.

Some of our family activities in this home:

_____

_____

_____

_____

In the box, write words, draw pictures, or scribble to show your feelings about moving:

Holidays!

What are you favorite holidays? Color the turkey and then describe your favorite holiday spent in your old home.

_____

_____

_____

My Favorite Spot

Paste a photograph or draw a picture of your favorite spot.

I loved this spot because:

_____

_____

_____

My Favorite Restaurant

Paste a photograph or draw a picture of the restaurant.

Describe the restaurant:

_____

_____

_____

_____

My Best Friend

Paste a photograph or draw a picture of your friends.

Write the name and address of your friend and three words to describe them:

_____

_____

_____

Pictures of Friends

Paste pictures here or draw a picture of you with your favorite people.

Keep in Contact

Fill out these cards and then cut them out to give to your friends so they can keep in touch with you!

Name:

_____

New address:

_____

_____

Email:

_____

Phone:

_____

Name:

_____

New address:

_____

_____

Email:

_____

Phone:

_____

Name:

_____

New address:

_____

_____

Email:

_____

Phone:

_____

Name:

_____

New address:

_____

_____

Email:

_____

Phone:

_____

Name:

_____

New address:

_____

_____

Email:

_____

Phone:

_____

Name:

_____

New address:

_____

_____

Email:

_____

Phone:

_____

Name:

_____

New address:

_____

_____

Email:

_____

Phone:

_____

Name:

_____

New address:

_____

_____

Email:

_____

Phone:

_____

Moving Crossword

```
S  S  L  T  C  P  S  E  A  Q  T  Y  X  W  E
U  X  E  T  E  T  J  G  M  R  F  F  E  P  G
M  N  V  N  O  X  N  A  O  Y  N  S  S  A  N
T  T  C  R  A  I  C  N  E  L  H  T  S  C  A
P  R  A  E  N  L  S  I  I  R  T  R  E  K  H
L  G  U  A  R  I  P  M  T  K  O  E  N  I  C
E  M  E  C  T  T  A  R  T  E  U  L  I  N  Q
O  L  D  I  K  F  A  E  I  O  D  O  P  G  Q
C  Q  O  X  V  S  P  I  M  A  Q  C  P  X  K
W  N  Y  R  F  R  I  E  N  D  S  A  A  D  E
E  R  U  T  N  E  V  D  A  T  S  T  H  B  K
S  S  E  N  D  A  S  L  K  L  Y  I  B  O  R
S  C  H  O  O  L  H  S  E  R  F  O  T  X  O
P  G  V  W  Z  W  R  E  J  T  H  N  R  E  W
S  W  R  M  V  C  P  E  N  F  T  G  S  S  Z
```

ADVENTURE	AIRPLANES	BOXES	CHANGE
CLEANING	EXCITED	EXPLORE	FAMILY
FRESH	FRIENDS	HAPPINESS	HOME
NEW	OLD	PACKING	RELOCATION
SADNESS	SCHOOL	SLEEP	STORAGE
TRANSITION	TRUCKS	UNCERTAINTY	WORK

My Old School

Paste a photograph or draw a picture of your school.

Describe your school:

_____

_____

_____

_____

My Former Teacher

Paste a photograph or draw a picture of your teacher.

Three things you like about your teacher:

_____

_____

_____

_____

Do you have a favorite toy or stuffed animal
that you take everywhere? What is it?

_____

_____

The City I Lived In!

Location: _____

People:_____

Country or state:_____

Leader:_____

Write five descriptive words about this

city or place:_____

_____

_____

Draw or paste a picture

Make (and sell) Lemonade

Think about people in your town who have less than you do. Can you fill a box of old toys and books to donate to them? How about doing a lemonade stand and donate all the money you make to a charity?

List some of your toys here that you would be willing to give away to a child in need.

_____

_____

_____

_____

_____

Make a List of Your Five Favorite Things about Living in your current home:

1. _____

2. _____

3. _____

4. _____

5. _____

What I will miss the most:

_____

_____

What I will miss the least:

_____

_____

_____

_____

Picture Page!

The Big Move

Pack your Box!

Don't forget your favorite things! Color the box and fill it with the most important things you plan to take with you!

Don't Forget

What do you plan to take with you that won't fit in a box? Draw pictures of people, pets, furniture, vehicles, and other favorite items here!

Transportation

How many forms of transportation will you use to get to your future home? Circle every form of transportation below.

TRAIN
CAR
BOAT
AIRPLANE
HELICOPTER
BICYCLE

OTHER: _____

Find Your Way Through the Maze!

First, draw a picture of your old and new homes!

Your Old Home

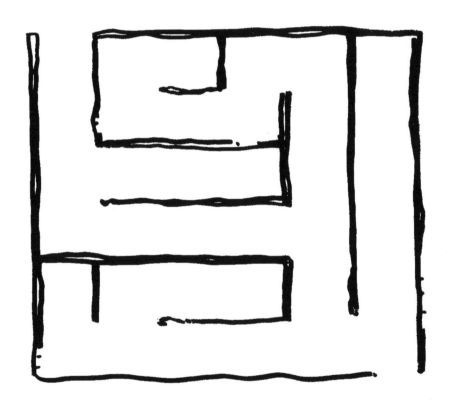

Your New Home

Pictures of Moving Day!
Add picture of packing, moving, or traveling!

Color the Moving Truck!

Exercise is Fun!

Moving can cause stress. Let it all out with some physical movement. Put a checkmark next to each activity that you complete.

_____ Do the Hokey Pokey but call it the "Moving Grooving!" Search for the music online for extra fun.

_____ Play hide and seek in your empty house or among the boxes.

_____ Musical Continents. Take packing tape and outline a globe on the empty floor. Put a box to represent each of the seven continents in the globe. Play music and when it stops you must grab a box. After each session, take one box away until only one person is left holding a box.

_____ Meditate. Find a quite place, make yourself as comfortable as possible, and try to empty your mind.

_____ Packing Basketball. Use boxes as hoops and rolled up packing paper as your balls.

_____ The Box Carry. Volunteer to carry as many boxes as you can downstairs. If you have parents or siblings, make it a contest to see who can move the most boxes in ten minutes.

_____ Ten Times Touch. Before leaving your house, run around as fast as you can and touch ten things that you loved.

_____ Dance party. Crank the music and dance as hard as you can for five minutes of every hour of work.

Take a little...leave a little

For this activity, find something very small that means something to you. It might be a coin, a special stone, or a piece of fabric with your initials on it. Find a secret place in your old home and tuck it in there as a way to leave a part of yourself behind.

Then, walk around your old house and town and find something special to take with you to your new home. You might find a stone, a flower to press in a book, or a beautiful leaf.

Inside the heart, list ideas of things to leave behind or take with you to your new home.

New Home

"Old home" means the home you are leaving. "New home" means the place where you are moving.

Important Information About Our New Home

Country

_____

Address

_____

Name of our Neighborhood

_____

Name of our School

_____

Favorite Place for Treats

_____

Favorite Food

_____

Favorite Park

_____

Favorite Family Friends

_____

Best Friend

_____

Favorite Smell

_____

Favorite Sight

_____

Favorite Sound

_____

Favorite Season

_____

KWL Chart

Fill in the first two columns before you move to your new home. Fill out the last column after you have been there for several weeks.

These are the things I KNOW about my new home.	These are the things I WANT to know about my new home.	This is what I LEARNED about my new home.

Draw a picture of what you might find beneath an airplane.

My New Home

Draw a map of your new home.

Describe your home:

_____

_____

_____

Map of My New Neighborhood

Country:

_____

City:

_____

Neighborhood:

_____

Street:

_____

My New Bedroom

Draw a map of your new bedroom.

Describe your bedroom:

_____

_____

_____

_____

Decorate your Room!

If you could decorate your room any way you wanted, what would it look like? Draw your room below. Add all the furniture and toys that would make this the perfect room for you.

My New School

Paste a photograph or draw a picture of your school.

Describe your school:

_____

_____

_____

_____

My New Teacher

Paste a photograph or draw a picture of your teacher.

Three things you like about your teacher:

_____

_____

_____

_____

Make New Friends

Fill out these cards and then cut them out to give to your new friends so they can arrange to get together!

Name:	Name:
_____	_____
New address:	New address:
_____	_____
_____	_____
Email:	Email:
_____	_____
Phone:	Phone:
_____	_____

Name:	Name:
_____	_____
New address:	New address:
_____	_____
_____	_____
Email:	Email:
_____	_____
Phone:	Phone:
_____	_____

Name:

_____

New address:

_____

_____

Email:

_____

Phone:

_____

Name:

_____

New address:

_____

_____

Email:

_____

Phone:

_____

Name:

_____

New address:

_____

_____

Email:

_____

Phone:

_____

Name:

_____

New address:

_____

_____

Email:

_____

Phone:

_____

My New City!

Location:

_____

People:_____

Country or state:_____

Leader:_____

Write five descriptive words about this

city or place:_____

_____

_____

Draw or paste a picture

Holidays for the Future!

Which holiday are you looking forward to celebrating in your new home the most? Draw a picture of a symbol or decoration associated with that holiday.

I am excited about these things for our new home:

_____

_____

_____

_____

The first three things I want to do in my new home include:

_____

_____

_____

My New House!
Paste or draw a picture of your new home.

Pictures of My New Friends

Paste pictures here or draw a picture of you with your new favorite people.

My goal for myself in my new home is:

_____

_____

_____

_____

Good Luck with Your Move!

Activity book by afterschoolplans.com

Illustrated by Cathy Stevens Pratt, Illustration, Design and Art
at catillustrates.com

Made in the USA
Middletown, DE
20 May 2015